To Gail &
~
friends

with love

Cathy
& Lazarus

I love my Cat

# I love my Cat

Georgina Harris

**CICO BOOKS**

LONDON NEW YORK

## Dedication
## To Steve

Published in 2011 by CICO Books
An imprint of Ryland Peters & Small
20–21 Jockey's Fields, London WC1R 4BW
519 Broadway, 5th Floor, New York, NY 10012

www.cicobooks.com

10 9 8 7 6 5 4 3 2 1

Text © Georgina Harris 2011
Design and illustration © CICO Books 2011

A CIP catalog record for this book is available from the
Library of Congress and the British Library.

ISBN: 978 1 907563 85 0

Printed in China

Editor: Dawn Bates
Design: David Fordham
Illustration: Trina Dalziel

# CONTENTS

# Your Companion Cat

"Time spent with CATS is NEVER wasted."

ATTRIBUTED TO SIGMUND FREUD (1856–1939),
PSYCHOANALYST

"**CATS** are the VISIBLE
soul of my home."

JEAN COCTEAU (1889–1963),
ARTIST, AND LOVER OF SIAMESE CATS

"**BEWARE**
of people who
dislike **CATS**."

IRISH PROVERB

# OFF THE RAILS?

Japan's FELINE stationmasters are known for their style and charm. In 2006, cost-cutting took place throughout the rail network. In the south, the Wakayama Electric Railway Company launched unmanned local stations, but hired a nominal stationmaster to keep an eye on the terminals. At Kishi station in Kinokawa, the town's grocer, Toshiko Kayama, got the job.

Mr Kayama, an ardent CAT-lover, soon started feeding the local strays after he had visited the station. Calico KITTY Tama was one. By the following year, Tama had gained access to the waiting room, where she greeted commuters morning and evening. Officially appointed in 2007, the rail network gave her an office from which to inspect the passengers. Tama's onsite meals were paid for by the rail company. Her office, which is now air-conditioned, was furnished with a basket and a ticket window.

In January 2008, Tama, to the delight of Kishi's residents, was promoted to the rank of "super stationmaster" by the mayor. The furry boss has two staff—Chibi and Miko, ginger tabbies. Tama and her assistants have generated over a billion yen for the rail company, and Tama has been the subject of a book and a documentary.

"**CATS** are magic creatures;
the more you cuddle them, the longer
you both live."

ANONYMOUS

"**A CAT** will be your
friend, but NEVER
your slave."

THÉOPHILE GAUTIER (1811–72), FRENCH
POET AND COMPANION OF MADAME THÉOPHILE,
A RARE GINGER QUEEN.
MADAME THÉOPHILE THIEVED FOOD FROM THE
DISTINGUISHED POET'S FORK DURING LITERARY DINNERS.
NONETHELESS, OR MAYBE BECAUSE OF HER SKILLS, SHE
FEATURED IN *MENAGERIE IN TIME* AND *SERAPHITA*, TWO
CELEBRATED COLLECTIONS OF 19TH-CENTURY POETRY.

"A MEOW heals the heart."

"A CAT makes a patch of grass in a SUNBEAM
welcoming in summer and
a fireside chair irresistible on a COLD night."

"Friendship with a CAT has just one risk: that of becoming a BETTER person."

ANONYMOUS

"LIKE clever people, CATS know instantly who **LIKES** or **DISLIKES** them—**UNLIKE** people, they don't care much."

ANONYMOUS

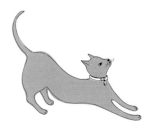

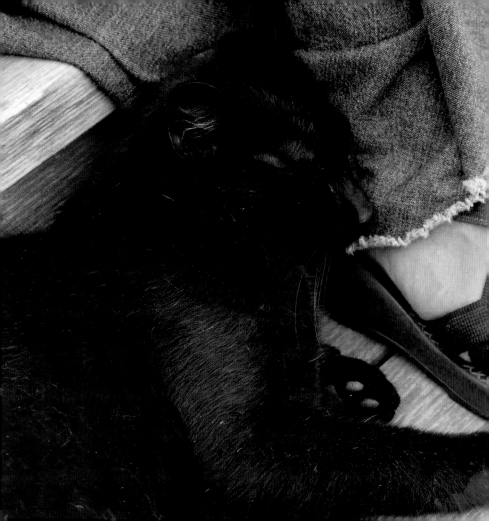

# MARMITE—THE *CAT* EVERYONE LOVES

Rescue CAT of the Year, "Moggy Midwife" Marmite won an award that made TV news headlines after helping his owner Lindsey during a difficult labor. Suffering with preeclampsia and anemia, mother-to-be Lindsey had spent most of her pregnancy resting, with black MOGGY Marmite curled up watchfully beside her.

Home alone one day, Lindsey went into labor—very fast. As she struggled with contractions, Marmite leapt into action as her birth partner; finally, Lindsey was rushed to hospital where she gave birth to a baby girl, Ruby. Lindsey said of her ordeal: "Marmite rubbed up against me and purred affectionately, which helped to distract me from the labor pains. He never once left my side and that was so reassuring.

"When I brought Ruby home, Marmite was thrilled to meet her—he is always guarding her and mews to let me know when she is crying. She is one very special CAT."

After a slumber,
The CAT yawns, rises and goes out
Looking for love.
Goes out,
Returns.

*THE LOVES OF A CAT*, KOBAYASHI ISSA (1763–1827), JAPANESE POET

"You will always be lucky if you know
how to make friends with strange CATS."

19TH-CENTURY AMERICAN PROVERB

"Something in the warmth of a CAT takes
the STING from solitude."

ENGLISH PROVERB

"No heaven will ever **heaven** be unless my CATS are there to welcome me."

ENGLISH FOLK RHYME

"The CAT and dog may kiss, but are none the better friends."

PROVERB, ANONYMOUS

# THE ROYAL CATS

IMPERIOUS, beautiful, and with a decidedly regal bearing, Marie Antoinette of France (1755–93) was accompanied through her trials in the French Revolution by her six best friends—a family of cloud-soft white CATS. Preparing to flee France and certain execution, the Queen ordered her furry friends to be stowed on the ship that she had hired to bear her to safety in America. But the ill-fated monarch never made it and, instead, faced the guillotine. However, the royal pets arrived in New York, where legend has it they are the ancestors of all today's pride of CAT fanciers, angora CATS.

# YOUR CHATTY CAT

Body language is the most natural—and frequent—way that your cat will communicate with you. CATS use their faces, tails, bodies, and paws to send you clear messages on a wide variety of subjects of daily interest—not just food and danger, but affection, trust, and family interaction. They love it when you "listen," so it pays dividends to recognize, and respond to, their affectionate, chatty signals. Overleaf are some of the most common ways your CAT tells you how he or she is feeling.

• Lying on her back: this is the ultimate signal of trust or submission. Displaying a furry belly shows your CAT is feeling playful, cuddly, and trusting.

• Face rubbing: this innate behavior, present from kittenhood, is a serious sign of acceptance. Your CAT is coating you with pheromones from her facial glands and saying, "This human is mine." Leg rubbing is another favorite, not least because it usually leads to cuddles and strokes.

● Tail straight up: a waving upright tail is a "Welcome Home" banner, homemade by your CAT.

● The look of love: looking up at you, and blinking, is your CAT'S way of telling you she cares. A direct gaze can be viewed as aggression, so a slow look and a blink says, "I won't attack, I'm comfortable with you." Some CATS like being blinked at—they find it relaxing.

• Meow: More so than humans, CATS speak for a reason. A meow is an alert, a reminder, a call to action, even a hopeful request. Always acknowledge your CAT'S meow, or answer verbally; you might be rewarded with a purr or a chirrup. If you hear a hiss, however, keep back; your CAT is annoyed.

• Tail down: Bad news—your CAT is feeling scared
or timid. Usually used to indicate the presence of
a stranger, whether human or feline, whom the CAT
is doubtful about. The crouched hind legs also reveal indecision.

# YOUR FUNNY CAT

"Dogs have owners,

CATS have staff."

ANONYMOUS

## "In a CAT'S eye, ALL THINGS belong to CATS."

ENGLISH PROVERB

"When I play with my CAT, who knows whether she is not amusing herself with me more than I am with her."

MICHEL DE MONTAIGNE (1533–92),
FRENCH PHILOSOPHER AND "OWNER" OF MADAME VANITY

"The CAT lives alone, has no need of neighbors, obeys only if it pleases her, feigns slumber so she can keep an eye on you, and shreds everything on which she lays a paw."

FRANÇOIS CHATEAUBRIAND, (1768–1848), FRENCH WRITER

# THE ALGONQUIN CAT

ONE of the world's ultimately chic, bohemian hotels, New York's Algonquin has been known for nearly a century for its rollcall of literary and artistic visitors, not least Dorothy Parker. But owner Frank Case saw another stylish Manhattan lady as his most honored guest—Matilda, the hotel CAT.

One night in the 1930s, a small, tired, hungry KITTEN stumbled into the hotel, in search of warmth and food. Without hesitation, hotelier Case extended his legendary hospitality to the needy stray, and since then the hotel has never been without its own furry "people-greeter." Current chatelaine Matilda monitors the arrival and departure of visiting celebs. Her birthday party, with 150 friends, is a fixture in New York's social diary, characterized by elegance and ceremony. However, the hotel admits that during the finale of the party in 2002, Matilda took a flying leap onto her custom-made cake, then fled, a trail of sugary paw prints decorating the Algonquin's famous dining room.

"It's for his own good that the CAT purrs."

IRISH PROVERB

"A CAT is more **intelligent** than people believe, and can be **taught** any crime."

*THE NOTEBOOK*, MARK TWAIN (1835–1910)

"CATS climb their way to the top.
That's why window treatments exist."

ANONYMOUS

"CAT obedience is meant to be a challenge.
I can't see it—my KITTY trained me in two days."

ANONYMOUS

"In order to keep check on your own IMPORTANCE,
get a dog that will worship you
and a CAT who ignores you."

ANONYMOUS

# THE FINE JUDGMENT OF THE FELINE

Tabby Sal, at the insistence of Suffolk Superior Crown Court in Boston, is the first CAT to be summoned for jury service. Anna Esposito, his owner, explained, "Sal is a member of the family so I listed him on the last census form under pets, but there has clearly been a mix-up."

She carefully wrote on behalf of Sal to confirm that he was "unable to speak and understand English," in the hope that her furry friend would be excused. But the court's jury commissioner insisted that Sal "must attend." Sal's veterinarian tried to help, stating the tabby is "a domestic short-haired neutered feline." The court did not budge—a judicial system website confirms jurors are "not expected to speak perfect English." This *is* a true story!

# YOUR INSPIRATIONAL CAT

"The smallest feline is a masterpiece."

LEONARDO DA VINCI (1452–1519)

# "A VERY FINE CAT INDEED."

—SAMUEL JOHNSON (1709–84) AND HODGE

Creator of the first dictionary of the English language, Samuel Johnson inspired awe in all, but not in his CAT, Hodge. Boswell, Johnson's biographer, noted: "I never shall forget the indulgence with which he treated Hodge, his CAT : for whom he himself used to go out and buy oysters, lest the servants having that trouble should take a dislike to the poor creature."

Sable-furred Hodge, who knew Boswell loathed CATS and deliberately mooched about making him uncomfortable, also knew who was boss. Boswell remembers: "I recollect him [Hodge] one day scrambling up Dr Johnson's breast, apparently with much satisfaction, while my friend smiling and half-whistling, rubbed down his back ... and when I observed he was a fine CAT, saying, 'Why yes, Sir, but I have had CATS whom I liked better than this,' and then, as if perceiving Hodge to be out of countenance, adding, 'but he is a very fine CAT, a very fine CAT indeed.'"

Hodge's statue, given by the City of London, stands outside Johnson's house in Gough Square, London EC4. Hodge is sitting on Johnson's famous dictionary, next to discarded oyster shells, above the inscription "a very fine CAT indeed." There is no statue of Johnson.

"Who amongst us doesn't
need the CAT'S power
to simply disregard the duties
of daily life and to relax?"

ANONYMOUS

"The key to CAT behavior:
when in doubt,
give it **attitude**."

ANONYMOUS

# CONVOY, THE WARTIME CAT HERO

As the Second World War raged through Europe, the Royal Navy kit suppliers had one special job—to make a tiny hammock for supply to HMS Hermione. The crew member who was to occupy it was the ship's CAT, Convoy, named for the sheer number of occasions when he led his ship on terrifying and dangerous missions. Listed in the ship's log, Convoy earned an active sailor's salary and received a full kit in miniature. But while the hammock may have proved tempting, Convoy never rested. He stood by his crew, his sailors, and his Captain to the bitter end. He was lost at sea with his crewmates, when Nazis torpedoed the Hermione in 1942.

"If animals could speak,
the dog would be a blundering
outspoken fellow, but the CAT would
have the rare grace of never saying
a word too much."

*THE NOTEBOOK*, MARK TWAIN (1835–1910)

# POLITICAL ANIMALS:
## DOWNING STREET _CATS_

Having rejected the US policy of an official first pet, London's Downing Street, residence of the UK prime minister, is, thanks to its age and size, an occasional retreat for the city's enterprising rats. Occasionally spotted at the base of newspaper photos, the rats are a gift to the UK's notorious tabloid press and headline writers, inspiring the well-loved English saying, "In London, you're never farther away than six feet from a politician."

But Downing Street does sometimes have its own Chief Mouser. Prime minister Margaret Thatcher was adopted by Humphrey, a large, fluffy, black-and white _CAT_, who stayed on to give several years of devoted service before retirement. Despite his calm, diplomatic air, Humphrey had a reputation for deserting his post to chase birds and slash at junior civil servants (but never the prime minister.) Now Larry, a canny tabby stray, has arrived to carry on the tradition.

**"The CAT'S motto:
LIFE IS HARD,
THEN YOU NAP."**

ANONYMOUS

**"Every dog has his day—
but night
is reserved for
the CAT."**

ANONYMOUS

# THE ANIMAL'S VICTORIA CROSS GOES TO
## SIMON THE CAT

Able seaman, Simon the CAT, of HMS Amethyst, was awarded the Dickin Medal, Britain's highest military honor for animals, in recognition of his unceasing gallantry during the post-Second World War Yangtze incident. Simon is the only CAT ever to be given the award. In 1949, as his ship and crew traveled through China, Simon, a black-and-white MOGGY, took his job seriously—he protected food on the ship from an infestation of unpatriotic rats. While his human crew battled attacks from Chinese Communists, and despite being badly wounded by shrapnel, Simon discharged himself from his sickbay to continue his successful war on rodents.

Simon's start in life was difficult and dangerous. Found wandering as a KITTEN stray in Hong Kong, he was rescued by one of the frigate's crew, and smuggled aboard. He proved to be a fine ratter, and, after a suitable probation period, became the official ship's CAT. He grew particularly fond of some sailors, gifting them a dead rat on their pillow and insisting on sleeping in the Captain's hat.

The siege was finally broken, and the Amethyst returned safely to Plymouth. Simon received a hero's welcome, and was later posthumously awarded the Dickin Medal for bravery. A fellow crew member said of him: "Simon's company and expertise as a rat-catcher were invaluable during the months we were held captive. During a terrifying time, Simon helped boost the morale of many young sailors, and is remembered with great affection."

## Picture credits

**Copyright © Cico Books**
Marl Lohman p1, pp2-3, p5 centre left, below right, p18, pp34-35, p36, pp38-39, p42, p50, p55, p60

**Copyright © Ryland Peters & Small**
Chris Everard p11, pp12-13, p27, p45, p53, p59; Chris Tubbs pp6-7, p9, p41, pp48-49, p56, p63, p64; Andrew Wood p5 above right, p25, pp32-33; Polly Wreford p17, p21; Francesca Yorke p14, pp46-47

**Used under licence from ShutterStock, 2011**
Tony Campbell p26, p30; Natalia D p28; M A Ertek p29 below; Eric Isselee p29, above; Kuban-girl p31; Miles Away Photography p22